Has God got a sense of humour ?

I THINK SO, LOOK AT SOME ANIMALS?

Or Elton on a bad day?

A FAMOUS QUOTATION

RICKY GERVAIS AT THE GOLDEN GLOBES.

Many speeches at the golden globes in Hollywood by the tv icon, left the audience in gasps of displeasure, he ridiculed his way through the Hollywood stars, the most privileged people on the planet.

REMEMBER HE SAID THEY ARE ONLY JOKES , WE ARE ALL GOING TO DIE SOON AND THERE IS NO SEQUEL.

When will he be nice…lol.?

WHY SO MANY GODS?

And what they believe?

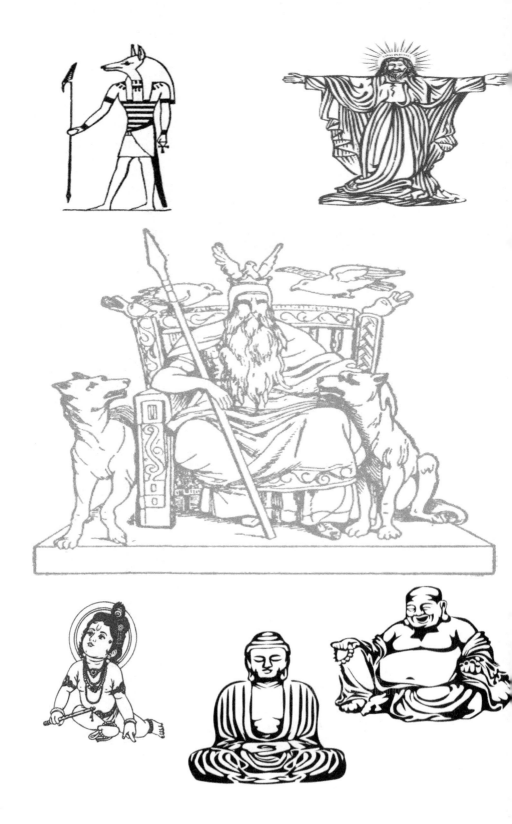

INTRODUCTION

WELCOME TO THE INTRODUCTION OF WHY SO MANY GODS AND WHAT THEY BELIEVE.

It is a mystery to why so many religions, how many people there are, that have their own god and the way they think of him, or her everyone assumes it's a male. whatever god it is and whatever they believe then it has been a big problem for mankind. It has also been a blessing in disguise, because the one thing most religions agree on is that it is better to live a good life than it is to live a bad life.

After this everything starts to fall apart, each religion has its own thinking and its own understanding. No wonder the ordinary people of the world, do not know what is what and who is who. And no bloody wonder if the religious people who are supposed to represent God on earth have no idea, then what hope has anyone else got? Not much, but in reality people who do not believe in God , believe in love. We all make mistakes and we all have different opinions, on everything. But we can all agree that love makes the world a happier place.

Religion has its place, but its gods have no power, if they had then there would be no killing and death. They defend this by saying that we go to heaven and God is testing us, or all sorts of reasonings? that when you think about it, do not add up to what love is. It is all a mess really the none believers know what love is, and those that believe in God do not know what love is. Because love does not point fingers. Repent or die, or go to hell, its hard enough this life , without thinking God has it in for you as well.

The Church of England.

Let us start with the easiest religion to understand , and the one that gives value for money, cob in the coin box a few coppers or notes and everything is ok. No pressure to go at any time it's up to you once a year, once a lifetime. Not bothered so long as some go and it keeps the vicar homed while he finds a better house.

The myth of the church of England was that king henry the 8th started the church. But in reality the catholic religion was formed from this, and henry the 8th decided if the pope could change it to Catholicism,(sounds a bit like alcoholism,) and change its doctrines then so could he.

 Henry wanted to get his leg over? and as today as was then the church, had a great say in all affairs. Henry declared he would put the church of England, under his own control and he would give it new doctrines.

Now henry was a man of the world, he liked his woman and he liked a good booze. So, he changed the religion to allow for all this, you can get married and then divorced. You can have a good old booze up and you do not upset the church of England's god. They noted that Jesus likes a party and changed water into wine when the off-licence was shut.

They had a quick flick through the bible, found some passages that say this ok and bobs your uncle, a new god, have a party and everyone's good to go. Their main belief is that if you are good you will go to heaven, and if you are bad you will go to hell.

Any more information than this , is beyond the church of England and let it stay that way.!

They know the passages for weddings and funerals etc, it's there bread and butter. Apart from that, the bible a mystery to them , that's great because too much knowledge can be bad.

IN THE WORLD OF GODS THESE ARE KNOWN AS.

THE DAZED AND CONFUSED.

THE LATTER DAY SAINTS.

(MORMONS)

Now this gets a bit more interesting, this religion is for the middle class edging to the upper class of people. It's not like c of e the working man's God, this god is a bit more difficult to please.

You have to be quite educated to understand what they are saying. they have taken things out of the bible, mixed it in with what joe smith said, added a bit of scientology a touch of Christianity. Mixed it all up together and they are still themselves trying to figure it out, it's called the book of Mormon.

It was started in 1872 by joseph smith, he found some golden plates with strange writing on, he was told to decipher the messages and to start a new and true religion.

The gold plates were never found , the myth of these plates and their location is still a mystery. Many scholars think Mr smith melted them down, stashed the money and later his ancestor Sam smith used this money for a good cause, and opened many drinking establishments, it is thought this god was trying to make friends with the working man's god . but as with all religion it is all a mystery.

Their god as I said before has a few more rules, and you must attend every so often, and sing songs and get baptised in water. If you are good or if you are bad, you get placed in different places the bad as always gets placed in hell.

But after that you get to half choose the destination depending on how good the worship is. You might be a worker and a lower grade of heavenly being, or you might be the overseer, or a chief adviser. Whatever your place is then you must do it. the ultimate goal is that you yourself will become the big cheese, you will be God himself,

You will have your own world and people to help or punish you decide. If like most religions you might want worship, the thing is your subjects will be under your control you will be God.

now a lot to understand and take in but the rewards are great. In the world of the gods these are known as

<u>THE MORONS, FROM OUTER SPACE</u>

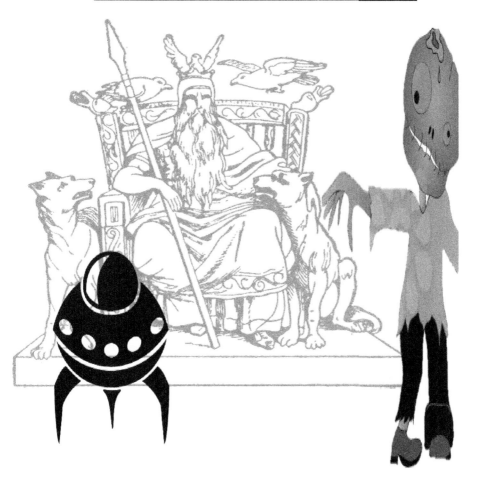

JEHOVAH'S WITNESS.

This religious group are know all over the world, the door knockers. Many jokes about this god, but fear is instilled from the word go. all other gods are not too fond of this one because they take business away.

You cannot get drunk, have a birthday party, or celebrate Christmas . this is just to name a few, the entry is easy so long as you believe what they are saying. It is quite expensive as you have to give a tithe etc, it is the same as the morons,, sorry Mormons.

They believe what a man told them about the bible, Charles Taze Russell. He sat down with his students and prayed over the bible to let it be understood. These out of everyone actually read the bible, but like all religion read too far and took to many things out of it to provide even more confusion.

The basic belief makes complete sense, if you are looking for it spiritually .but it all breaks down when you put love to it, it makes sense but shows no love.

They believe that the creator made everything, he put Adam and eve on the earth, then they went against God and buggered it up for the rest of us. The world turned bad so the creator sent a flood for a fresh start and saved a few people. There also was a war in heaven and we got stuck with Satan, he was cast down to earth. And that is why all the trouble, we are the dumping ground for all gods shit.

 The creator however sent his son to show us how to live Jesus, they believe when he returns that he will kill bad people and save good people. What they fail to understand is that Jesus is not a killer and God is not a killer.

The clue is in his job title, the creator not the killer , because this god is fearsome , he is mistaken at times for Satan. And many horror movies have been made about his temper.?

THE DERANGED AND THE DELUDED.

THE CATHOLIC RELIGION.

This one has a woman as its god, I think because the other gods are men , then let's give the girl ago. Like I said earlier the church of England was the first founded religion and then later it was changed to Catholicism, then henry wanted a bonk and changed it back to c of e. that is why a lot of characteristics of both gods and beliefs interlock.

One God is a man and one God is a woman so that is why they keep arguing they do however sometimes get together for a beer ,at the Sam smiths pub just to show support for the Mormons god, or just might be checking the competition.

The main beliefs of the Catholics, again it's like the church of England if you are good you go to heaven and if you are bad you go to heaven. If you do sin then they have a special counter, called a rosery bead. It's like touching wood if you are superstitious. They are not too sure on the bibles sayings, somebody read it once or so they believe and what they do not understand they make it up.

Their god is not that bad a god , again heaven ,,hell awaits but in general he leave people alone, worship don't worship not sure really. But it keeps people happy , apart from the vicar or priest they marry the building, they cannot marry a human. This is a bit strange, so I think that's why they like a beer.

But this is great because it makes life fun, this god will get drunk with you and have a fag and smoke and swear. So great value for money, just a few bob now and then, they are the wealthiest of the gods but the evangelists are catching up. At least with this religion the money does go to the top, again buying up the rooms for gods house.

A good preaching system of love and forgiveness helps them to come across well. These are known in the hall of the gods as.

THE ROLLER BEADERS.

Lets just have a beer , Jesus likes a pint he turns water into wine when he runs out , a good old boy.

SCIENTOLOGY.

Now then, now we are talking, scientology it says it all in the name, you need a degree to understand it, money, or fame to join it and believe in fairies of sorts. they do have lower dominions for the working class but it will still cost you.

Value for money very expensive and very time consuming, you have to be hooked up to a special machine that measures your wavelength, I think that's what they measure, this might be a secret word for something else not sure, but anyway if its big enough you're in.

They believe that your spirit is eternal and that the body is its vehicle. The spirit is called a thetan and we are the carriers of this spirit, my spirit I carry is called jack Daniels we all have our own spirit to bear, some have a cross.

The good thing is that these people do not believe in a deity or creed etc, you have to make your own decisions on your choice of God. This is great because it's like all gods rolled into one major god. Hollywood is connected to this religion, and that makes sense because in Hollywood , whoever lives their wants to be the biggest and best, so many gods here take your pick. That's why it is the 2nd most expensive god in creation. But as the world knows you get what you pay for, and if nothing else you have the chance to ride in a spaceship.

It was started by a man called, L. Ron Hubbard in the 1950s , he was an author of scientific books and publications. His books were not selling to well then all of a sudden they took off, and the momentum of science fiction and God became one.

He made lots of money and he has a steady fan base now all around the globe and he is hoping soon to venture to space. in the hall of the gods these are.

THE CRAZY GANG.

EVANGELISTS.

This god of the evangelists is a money god the most richest preachers in the world are evangelists. Value for money none really they tell you what you can read for free and charge you for it. but they do tell you how to acquire money and freedom, it's a franchise from there God who knows all about money and the power of it.

this god will not take just some money of you, he will take all you have and you will give it freely, its brilliant the best pyramid scam in the world. All they say is we are keeping it safe for when God comes to collect it, that's why all the cars and houses , it says in the bible god has many rooms he will have now the evangelist are buying them all.

They do however in between stockbrokers and banking etc. preach out of the bible, Jesus is the mascot and their motto is….

"IT IS BETTER TO GIVE THAN RECEIVE."

Its bloody brilliant, tell people what they want to hear, charge them for it, say God forgives you and a better life awaits. And money is the route of all evil, so let us look after it for you.

This god is a major player he knows how to stack the chips. No come back on the preachers, God told me to do it, and this diamond bracelet was given to me as a thank you for services rendered. I cannot really tell you what they believe because it is so divers. But the main teaching is how to do the biggest con the world has ever seen and get away with it, because it's all in the name of Jesus. Jesus loves you halleluiah, 50 bucks please.

Your sins are forgiven hallelujah 100 bucks please , what about going to heaven?.. (HOW MUCH YOU GOT?).

They believe in money? in the world of gods these are known as.

THE MONEY KINGS

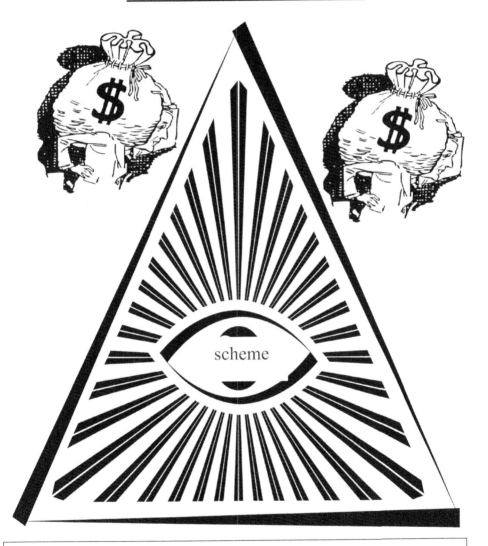

scheme

The only pyramid scam that will never run out of money.

THE QUAKERS.

Now the quakers, to me an amazing bunch of people and there God is most powerful, or it would be if they had one. they believe in the power of love, and a god sort of spirit.

This god is real value for money he does not want anything, this god will give you money. What about that then, every business that a quaker has founded shares its money among its employees. They do something few other religions do, they practice what they preach and show it in all ways. They do not worship a god, but in reality they worship the true god, love.

This religion has mainly 2 divisions, kind of like labour and conservatives, they are just like these 2 parties only these 2 parties don't fall out, they come to an understanding. Unlike our bloody lot, and if anyone has something to say they always listen reason things out and make a decision on evidence provided.

They do believe in Jesus Christ and take his teachings as a guideline. They search for enlightenment a bit like the Buddhist monks do, without the need to chant. they strongly believe that in mankind there is good and God in everyone, they do not have a main worshiping theme like most religions they believe in letting the spirit flow, the Catholics like the quakers because they to like letting the spirit flow, like vodka or whiskey. and this is there form of worship, it differs a lot from other religions as they are saying do as I do not as I say.

So, if you can get in with these people, and have no job or life is getting you down, then at the moment they get full marks of me for they will help you find your way, without repayment.

As you can see their beliefs are a bit like porridge , it can be eaten any time of day but best in the mornings to keep you warm just like there God or no god ? , but the idea of love is there its heart warming.

(not sure what ive just said but , it won't matter they are quakers)

In the hall of the gods these are known as

THE PORRIDGE MAKERS

GO COMPARE A GOD .COM

GOCOMPAREAGOD@GMAIL.COM

IT IS IMPORTANT TO KNOW WHAT IS ON OFFER.

THIS IS THE ONLY WEBSITE THAT GIVES YOU THE BELIEFS OF EVERY RELIGION.

TRY BEFORE YOU BUY THAT'S OUR MOTTO.

A GOD TO SUIT, EVERY OCCASION AND POCKET.

WHICH GOD OFFERS VALUE FOR MONEY , OR WORSHIP. WHAT IS REQUIRED OF YOU TO PLEASE THE DEITY?

GO, COMPARE A GOD.

Now then, I have come up with an idea that would save a lot of time when you are thinking of joining a god. Most people wait for a knock at the door and this gives them opportunity to say that God sent them. And before anyone knows it a few quid gone and if you leave, you go against God. So, I am setting up go compare your god.

WE WILL BE HAVING STAR RATINGS, AND FEEDBACK.

Customer reviews, and any special offers in the pipeline. What their god expects of you and also how often he needs worship. It is very important to get these things right at the start.

We will be giving prizes for most things.

We will have a god of the week prize,, church of the year prize and also most new members prize.

Also, easy and understandable charts, money in bank how many souls saved, how many marked for destruction.

Best interpretation of scripture award,

Best newcomer, most attendance etc.

We will also provide a league table like in football, a premier division for loaded churches, a champions league for mainstream and lower leagues for cults.

Like in all forms of life, we need to know before we buy into anything, and this is important. We could also do a free weeks trial, try before you buy scheme, and best miracle of the month, award, winner takes all .

JUST A SHORT READ.

A nice little walk-through religion, not a lot of information just enough to help you decide if you want to join any of these clubs.

The extended paperback book offers more insight and features of up-and-coming new beliefs and religions.

There are some promising new gods on the horizon. But as with all new businesses, some will fold and some will succeed. The long-established churches have a firm grip. The evangelist will buy them up most likely.

SO, WHO WILL BE GOD OF THE YEAR FOR 2024?

If you or anyone you know, wants to nominate a god or religion for this prestigious award, voting instructions will be announced later in the year.

August will see the start of our new event, come try a god. It's like a car boot sale but indoors, vicars and preachers etc will each have their own stall and offers .hopefully all the big names will be there, bring some spare change and entry will be £5.00.

No one should be afraid to come and browse, we have strict rules on heavy selling. And security in case of in fighting.

New startups welcome, all invited so bring your bible bring your god and winner takes all. The thing is it's a great day out, bring the family see what's on offer and make an educated decision.

LAST YEARS WINNER WAS LOVE.

WHAT IS LOVE?

Love is kind and generous, love holds your hand and love hugs you when you are feeling upset. Love takes care of you and sends you on your way happy. Love cries with you and it laughs with you love wants to be your best friend.

Love always looks out for your interests, love will do whatever it takes to keep you safe. It applauds when it sees good deeds and it is sad with bad deeds.

Love will not get puffed up or angry, love understands everything. Love listens and agrees and then only tells you its opinion if it will help.

Love knows what to do in any situation , it thinks it reasons and it learns .love loves everything and everybody, because it only sees the good in people.

Love hates as well, love hates it when people die, or when people cry. It hates to see killing and sadness and love will not boast, love will die for you and not want any thanks because love loves you .love is everywhere, it takes its child to school. It works hard to keep its family, it tells its mum and dad how much they mean , and it loves its children. Love makes mistakes but always says sorry.

Love is the nearest thing to perfection. Because love makes everything perfect.

THE AWARDS for 2023.

Now the awards for 2023, after looking at most religions and reasoning out the bible .then in my opinion these are the awards.

Richest religion to date……………..CATHOLIC CHURCH.

Most worshippers…(mainstream)………..CHRISTIANITY.

Richest preachers………………………….EVANGELISTS.

Most confusing…..……………,………….SCIENTOLOGIST.

Best value for money………,…...CHURCH OF ENGLAND.

Hardest religion to please…… ….JEHOVAH'S WITNESS.

Offering the most…(get to be a god)…...THE MORMONS.

THE QUAKERS GOD

(This god takes the front seat, with his principles)

This god and faith, beats every other god hands down these people have understood the bible and God. They have taken away from it all the good and left the bad behind. They share if you want a few bob they will lend it you. They always look for the good in people, no real worship involved. They rejoice in truth and allow for other people's views. No real hardship , just do good, anything that goes against love they won't look at. They move with the times, you don't have to dress like Charles dickens anymore .well done the quakers.

NOW FOR SOME SERIOUS STUFF?

Ok the fun stops now, i sound religious just in those few words, if anyone reading this is offended why? Has God not got a sense of humour is not the spirit of God joy and happiness.

You see ive had a bit of fun at religions expense and why not, its all very confusing to the man on the street, follow us repent or die is the motto, come worship or face the flames of hell.? All I can say is b""locks to you, which god do we follow which religion?

Religions are in a powerful place and no wonder no one has much faith in them, if they can not agree on anything how can ordinary sinners believe anything. The biggest lie ever told was there is only one God, you better tell the crazy gangs this. here is a list of what each god has in store for you.

1..........one will send you to heaven

2.........one will send you to hell

3..........one will let you live on earth forever

4.........one will make you a god

5..........one will make you a spaceman

And this is just a few beliefs of God, so how many gods are there it's not one. The bible itself tells us there are many gods but only one true god and that god is not a god , its love. But that's my interpretation of truth, others crave revenge and judgement who am I, to go against goliath?

If you take the good stuff only that each religions offer then you can see a truth.?

THE GOOD STUFF.

Now then out of all this confusion religions throw at us , there has got to be some good points and sound reasonings.? The bible says always look for the good so lets do this and reason .

First Jehovah's witness , they mainly believe that we can live on earth forever, this would make sense. Why , well why make earth and then a heaven to live in? the earth and the universe is vast just incase no ones noticed, so let's put that down.

Next c of e , church of England , if you are good you go to heaven if you are bad hell, now heaven to live in is scrubbed because we removed that its nonsense. But where you are born could be heaven or hell this is true imagine being born in the holocaust as a Jew.? Or Ukraine now or the Gaza strip.? Also imagine being the sultan of Bruni or bill gates that has servants and maids and all your dreams come true,? So, heaven and hell is on earth.

Next the Catholics preach we all go to heaven because God loves us all and we are all forgiven. Now again dump heaven to live in think of it as more of a feeling, good thinking, and good emotions like love, this is heaven spiritually, the bible does say the kingdom of God is not visible this would make sense …love., just remove evil.

Scientology believes we have an immortal soul that lives forever it just takes on different vessels. So, let's keep this because its one thing they believe that makes sense , the bible says we have a soul, so out with the testing machine and in with a sensible reasoning.

CONTINUED.

The evangelists, now it's a bit hard finding there truth its so diverse , but money and Jesus walk hand in hand with this religion. Lets remove the dosh of the table and concentrate on Jesus. A good man who gave his life for mankind this is love ,so lets put love in the mix , why? Because love never fails it hopes all things and believes all things, and if we do this we can get to the truth of things. The truth is very important to us as the truth will set us free.

Now the quakers , the winners of God of the year 2023 these people are amazing in there beliefs and lives. They take into account all beliefs and ridicule none, they believe there is a better way to live and to always look for the good in people, they put all other religions to shame. They don't take from anyone they give and they believe God dwells in all humans and this god is love. They discuss and agree by majority they don't door knock and tell you to believe them or die, they promote love and understanding, so let's put down God dwells in all and manifests as love.

Now the Morons , sorry the Mormons this religion has a few beliefs but the main one is to be a god, live like a god and be a god. Every belief has some reasoning from the bible and this one is no exception. The bible says that we are all gods and that when we understand this we can set ourselves free from death. So, this one stays in death is not to good.

Well, that's just a few beliefs sorted and truths , the bible says to be humble and share and believe all things.?

THE TRUTHS LEARNED

1....we can live on earth forever.

2....heaven is a feeling.

3....heaven and hell are on earth.

4....God is love and dwells in everyone.

5....we die but the spirit lives on.

6....we are all gods.

So, there we have just a few truths gleaned from religions, no revenge or judgement in these truths, just information that makes sense. Some good news for a change , its funny Jesus said spread the good news. I am not to sure if religions understand that revenge and judgement and worship are not good news.

Coming soon is more of the truth gleaned again from other religions , I hope you have smiled while reading my book , you see God is a spirit of joy and he has a sense of humour without doubt.

You see the world needs simple understandings to bring it together , not sermons without end or repent or die. These things just bring about fear if I know anything Mr Gervais will be right with his final words of wisdom.?

REPENT OR DIE.?

Repent or die is the most valuable information in the bible and religions think repentance is of sin? No, it is not of sin , Jesus came and died so the slate is wiped clean, to not believe this, is to not believe in Jesus and we know what religions say if you don't believe?

You see to believe in Jesus is to believe in what he stood for love and forgiveness, if you believe in love is better than evil , his work is done.

Reason it out , many people would die for there children or loved ones , now a sacrifice as big as this covers all mankind. To say if you only believe puts conditions on Jesus sacrifice and Jesus love is unconditional.

That's why repentance is the key to life and understanding of the bible and God. It is to repent of false beliefs and find the truth , repent ! turn to each other and see the writing on the wall as scripture pointed out.

For God loved the world he gave his only sun

FORGIVENESS VOUCHER

I PROMISE TO PAY THE BEARER A BUCKET FULL OF FORGIVENESS AND LOVE.

REDEEMABLE ANYTIME AND ANYWHERE

FOR AND ON BEHALF OF THE ALMIGHTY

The ancient of days

NO TERMS OR CONDITIONS ATTACHED.

CONCLUSION.

So, there we have just a few examples of what each religion believes, there are many gods and many beliefs. Every person in the entire world can believe whatever they want to. It is up to each and every person to decide their own truth. We all live and we all die by what we believe, we all believe that we will die and we do.

None of the religious groups can agree on much? And that is up to them, in truth they are just clubs that have found a book and taken away what they want to take away and added to it what they want to add to it. it says in the bible be careful of what you add to this book or take away from it, and when you look at the world that seems to be true confusion abounds.

Ive tried to find something that you could take away from this book, and something that believers and none believers could agree on, and if the book was closed and shut, and handed back to God .and we said don't leave your bloody book lying around again, we cannot understand it. the only thing that makes sense in it is love, we don't understand you. I am sure he would reply oh, I am love, when you understand what love is you will understand me.

Everyone alive can agree that love is better than evil, believers and none believers can agree on this. anyone alive can agree that love is good. But that is all I can find in each religion and in each belief of mankind, it's the only thing we can all agree on, if the world had more love then the world would be a better place. So, the only sensible conclusion to come to about religion and the bible is this.

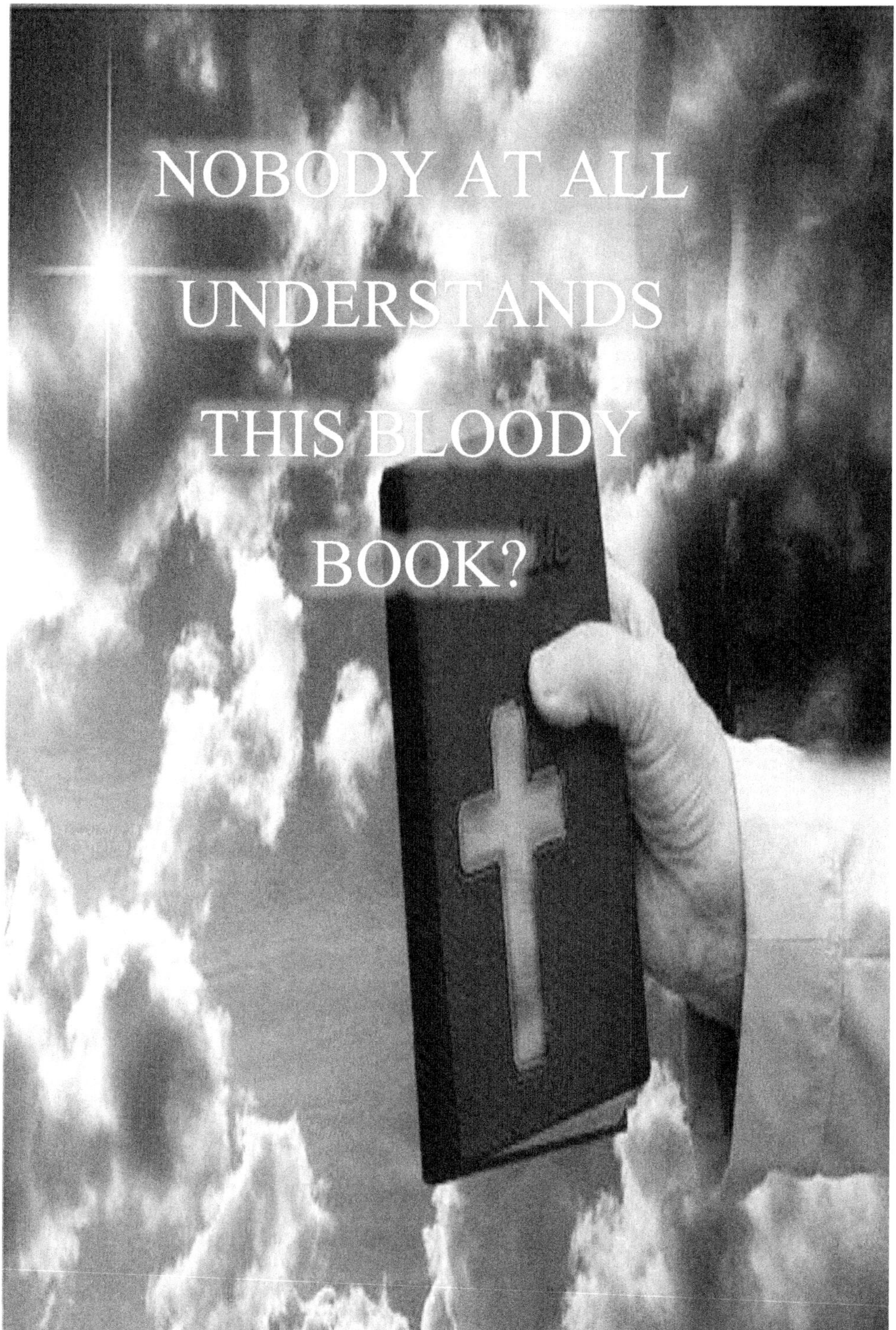
NOBODY AT ALL
UNDERSTANDS
THIS BLOODY
BOOK?

The Bible Is Confused.

IT MUST BE
NOBODY CAN
AGREE ON IT.
WRITTEN BYMAN,
INSPIRED BY GOD
AND MIXED UP BY
THE DEVIL.
This is the only possible
answer.

IT IS A POLYSEME?

In one of the more extreme polysemous developments, a word can take on an opposite meaning, as dust (v.) can mean to clean up small particles (dust the furniture) or to apply small particles (dust the Birthday cake with powdered sugar) Polysemy is the **association of one word with two or more distinct meanings**,

and a polyseme is a word or phrase with multiple meanings. The word "polysemy" comes from the Greek for "many signs." The adjective forms of the word include polysemous or polysemic. In contrast, a one-to-one match between a word and a meaning is called "monosemy."

THIS BOOK HAS MANY MEANINGS, BUT ONLY ONE TRUTH.

IN THE BIBLE THERE ARE 3 STORY'S.

1st story is mythical and spiritual.

2nd story is the true story of creation and links to reality.

3rd story is a new story ready to be lived.

PROMOTION.

OUR HISTORY IS FAKE
Scan the code to see all books in
the series.

COMING SOON MYSTERY OF THE SOUP.

ALL I CAN TELL YOU IS THE TRUTH, THEN IT IS UP TO YOU?

And The True Truth Makes Sense.

I am going to tell you three words that explain the whole truth. Then I will explain how I came to know.

THE THREE WORDS THAT EXPLAIN ANY QUESTION.

LOVE ....HATE.........SOUP?

See it is as easy as 1,2,3,

But why soup? Soup is a <u>polysemy</u> word.

(It has many meanings)

SOUP IT CAN MEAN ANYTHING

Thetruth737@Outlook.Com.

THE ANSWERS ARE BLOWING IN THE WIND.

Copy link to see author page and all books.

Amazon.co.uk: THE ORACLE: Books, Biography, Blogs, Audiobooks, Kindle

Or type in search fact or fiction truth or lie. Click on author title and it will take you direct to the bookstore.

More free stuff or buy for a pound, and the truth shall set us free, lets prove the truth and be free.

LOVE IS ALL THAT MATTERS, AND WE ALL HAVE SOME OF THAT.

THE LAST WORDS FROM A MODERN-DAY PROPHET

Ricky Gervais one of the funniest men alive today , he is quick witted and very funny, some might not agree but he has no fear, even God says do not be afraid. Ricky says its not rocket science if you don't like the humour stay away.

He has reasoned out the god of religions and he stands by what he says , what you have to understand about this man is he is a man with his own thinking and reasoning ability, he puts it to good use and only says what people are thinking.?

He knows the bible and God more than religions do, he is not scripturally shy , he reads then reasons, nothing wrong in that, ive listened to some of his jokes on Noah's arc etc and they are funny. I bet God himself is laughing his knob of, if he had a knob he is spirit not flesh , religions nailed his body to a tree.

Anyway, Ricky was asked what if God is real and you meet him what do you think would happen and he gave the most knowledgeable and spiritual answer yet, and it's the truth, he said.

"GOD WILL FORGIVE ME , BECAUSE ITS GODS FAULT FOR MAKING ME AN ATHEIST.?"

IN TRUTH, ITS NOT GODS FAULT ITS CONFUSIONS FAULT FOR CAUSING CONFUSION.?

COMING SOON.

WHY SO MANY GODS

VOLUME 2.

THE TRUTH SHALL

SET US FREE.

More hilarity as we find truth and search for the answers in some more religious beliefs.

Coming soon the humdingers?

Awakening is not changing who you are, but discarding who you are not.

Printed in Great Britain
by Amazon